YOUR KNOWLEDGE HAS VALUE

Syed Asaduzzaman

Coating of Yarns with Electro-active Layers

GRIN Publishing

Bibliographic information published by the German National Library:

The German National Library lists this publication in the National Bibliography;
detailed bibliographic data are available on the Internet at http://dnb.dnb.de .

Imprint:

Copyright © 2015 GRIN Verlag GmbH
Print and binding: Books on Demand GmbH, Norderstedt Germany
ISBN: 978-3-656-96795-8

This book at GRIN:

http://www.grin.com/en/e-book/298648/coating-of-yarns-with-electro-active-layers

GRIN - Your knowledge has value

Since its foundation in 1998, GRIN has specialized in publishing academic texts by students, college teachers and other academics as e-book and printed book. The website www.grin.com is an ideal platform for presenting term papers, final papers, scientific essays, dissertations and specialist books.

Visit us on the internet:

http://www.grin.com/

http://www.facebook.com/grincom

http://www.twitter.com/grin_com

Coating of Yarns with Electro-active Layers

MA Projects Winter Semester 2014/15

Syed Asaduzzaman

Contents

2

Abstract

Recently electrically conductive textiles have been of increasing research interest due to their numerous possibilities for application in various fields of activity. These conductive textiles in future will be used in clothing to measure body parameters or in textiles used to protect against electromagnetic shielding. As this is an emerging field, there is still a lack of characterizing and evaluating the performance of these conductive materials. In the scope of this project work, different yarn materials are coated with Polypyrrole and Carbon (Graphite). These layers are applied to realize textile humidity and temperature sensors. Coated yarns are characterized in order to evaluate their behavior when being worn in every-day life. So, Literature study on electro-less coating of textile structures with Polypyrrole and Carbon (Graphite) coating of different yarn materials and Characterization of coated yarns is presented in this project work.

Keywords: Coating, polypyrrole, Carbon (Graphite), dip coating, diameter, resistance, conductivity.

Chapter I
Literature Study

1.1 Coating

A layer of a substance spread over a surface for protection or decoration; a covering layer. Fabrics made of conventional textile materials generally have high electrical resistivity ($> 10^{10}$ Ω). Treatment with a conducting polymer lowers the surface resistivity to ($1–10^4$ Ω). Unfortunately, conducting polymers have a poor level of process ability because of their mechanical and physical properties (e.g. fragility, infusibility and insolubility). These problems have been overcome by deposition of conducting polymer. [11]

1.2 Polypyrrole (PPy)

- Polypyrrole (PPy) is a type of organic polymer formed from by polymerization of Pyrrole.

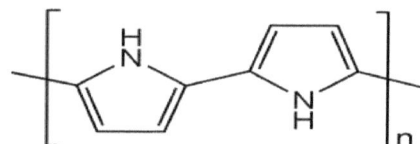

Figure 1: Polypyrrole Chemical Structure [10]

- Among the many electrically conductive polymers that have been given attention to over the last decade, Polypyrrole (PPy), which consists of five membered heterocyclic rings, has become especially important because of it exhibits high conductivity, low resistivity, redox properties, easy preparation with low cost and environmental stability. [10]

1.3 Coating of Yarns with Polypyrrole (PPy)

There are different possible ways or methods available to coat the yarns with Polypyrrole. Like:

Cotton yarn can be coated with Polypyrrole by the

- *Vapor Phase Polymerization* Technique
- *Synthesized via Chemical Processing Route*

Wool yarns can be coated with Conducting Polypyrrole by the

- *Chemical Synthesis Method*
- *Vapor Polymerization*

Nylon yarns can be coated with Polypyrrole by the

- *Chemical Polymerization*
- *Vapor Polymerization*

Polyester yarns can be coated with Polypyrrole by the

> *Chemical Synthesis Method* [11] [8]

1.3.1 Applications of Polypyrrole Coated Yarns

Since Polypyrrole shows extremely low thermal diffusivities regardless of the electrical conductivity, the low thermal conductivity gives significant advantage.

- These textiles are suitable for several applications from antistatic films to electromagnetic interference shielding devices and sensors.
- The usage of conductive polymers in electromagnetic shielding applications is widespread.

Other applications are:

- Antibacterial fabrics
- Wearable sensors in Biomechanical monitoring. [11] [7]

1.4 Carbon

Carbon has a symbol C and atomic number 6. It is nonmetallic and tetravalent — making four electrons available to form covalent chemical bonds. There are three isotropic forms of carbon as ^{12}C and ^{13}C being stable, while ^{14}C is radioactive, decaying with a half-life of about 5,730 years.

There are several allotropes of carbon of which the best known are graphite, diamond, and amorphous carbon. [5]

1.5 Graphite

Graphite is made almost entirely of carbon atoms. Graphite is the most stable form of carbon under standard conditions. Therefore, it is used in thermochemistry as the standard state for defining the heat of formation of carbon compounds. Graphite may be considered the highest grade of coal, just above anthracite and alternatively called meta-anthracite, although it is not normally used as fuel because it is difficult to ignite. [6]

Figure 2: Microscope Image of
Graphite Surface Atom [6]

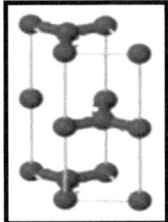

Figure 3: Graphite's
Unit Cell [6]

6

Graphite has a layered, planar structure. In each layer, the carbon atoms are arranged in a honeycomb lattice with separation of 0.142 nm, and the distance between planes is 0.335 nm. The two known forms of graphite, *alpha* (hexagonal) and *beta* (rhombohedral), have very similar physical properties, except the graphene layers stack slightly differently. The hexagonal graphite may be either flat or buckled. The alpha form can be converted to the beta form through mechanical treatment and the beta form reverts to the alpha form when it is heated above 1300 °C. [6]

1.5.1 Properties

Graphite and graphite powder are valued in industrial applications for their self-lubricating and dry lubricating properties. There is a common belief that graphite's lubricating properties are solely due to the loose interlamellar coupling between sheets in the structure. However, it has been shown that in a vacuum environment (such as in technologies for use in space), graphite is a very poor lubricant.

The electrical properties of these conductive materials are influenced by different factors such as the carbon black concentration, and the insertion of conductive yarns in the fabric. An increase in CB particle concentration from 10.41% to 15.96% causes a decrease in electrical resistivity we can say that increasing the CB particle concentration causes a decrease in electrical resistivity; the concentration of the other components of the coating material have less of an influence on the electrical properties of the conductive fabric obtained. [17]

1.5.2 Applications Carbon (Graphite) Coated Yarns

Conductive fabrics represent potential applications for instance;

- ✓ In clothing
- ✓ In the medical and military fields as
  - * Sensors
  - * Actuators
  - * Electromagnetic shields etc.

Conductive textiles obtained using conductive materials can be used in

- ✓ Heating applications where parts of the body can be heated
- ✓ In health care and
- ✓ Military applications. [11]

1.6 Dip Coating

Dip coating refers to the immersing of a substrate into a tank containing coating material, removing the piece from the tank, and allowing it to drain. The coated piece can then be dried by force-drying or baking. It is a popular way of creating thin film coated materials along with the spin coating procedure.

Stages of Dip Coating

The dip coating process can be, generally, separated into 3 stages:

- **Immersion**: the substrate is immersed in the solution of the coating material at a constant speed preferably judder free.
- **Dwell time**: the substrate remains fully immersed and motionless to allow for the coating material to apply itself to the substrate.
- **Withdrawal**: the substrate is withdrawn, again at a constant speed to avoid any judders. The faster the substrate is withdrawn from the tank the thicker the coating material that will be applied to the board. [1]

1.7 Electrical Conductivity

It is the degree to which a specified material conducts electricity, calculated as the ratio of the current density in the material to the electric field which causes the flow of current. Electrical conductivity is the ability of a material to carry the flow of an electric current (a flow of electrons). [2]

1.8 Electrical Resistance

Another way of describing the conductivity of a material is through resistance. Resistance can be defined as the extent to which a material prevents the flow of electricity. Silver, aluminum, iron and other metals have a low resistance (and a high conductivity). Wood, paper, and most plastics have a high resistance (and a low conductivity).

The unit of measurement for electrical resistance is called the ohm (abbreviation: Ω). The ohm was named for German physicist Georg Simon Ohm (1789–1854), who first expressed the mathematical laws of electrical conductance and resistance in detail. This choice of units clearly illustrates the reciprocal (opposite) relationship between electrical resistance and conductivity. [2]

1.9 Plasma Treatment

If a substrate has a low surface energy, its wettability is poor and coating adhesion very scarce, and then needs a surface treatment to increase energy. The surface energies of the treated materials increased substantially, thereby enhancing wettability, printability, and adhesion properties.

The Plasma Treatment Process consists of exposing a polymer to a low-temperature, high density glow discharge. Primarily, a plasma treatment provides manifold possibilities to refine a polymer surface, enabled by the adjustment of parameters like gas flows, power, and pressure and treatment time.

The resulting plasma is a partially ionised gas consisting of large concentrations of excited atomic, molecular, ionic, and free-radical species which force themselves into the polymer and roughens the surface of the polymer (yarn). Plasma treatment of polymer surfaces causes not only a modification during the plasma exposure, but also leaves active sites at the surfaces which are subject to post-reactions. [16]

1.10 Materials Used

In the scope of this project we have used four different types of yarns manufactured from synthetic materials. Such as:

- ✓ **Polyamide 6.10**; Diameter: **0.220 mm**
- ✓ **Polyester PET 930C**; Diameter: **0.550 mm**
- ✓ **Polyester PETP Monofilament**; Diameter: **0.650 mm**
- ✓ **Polyester PET 930R Monofilament**; Diameter: **0.650 mm**

Chapter II
Coating of Yarns with Polypyrrole

2.1 Polypyrrole (PPy) Coating Procedure

2.1.1 Plasma Treatment

As yarns used for this project work are synthetic and have low coating adhesion so plasma treatment has done.

The Plasma Treatment Process consists of exposing a polymer to a low-temperature, high density glow discharge. Primarily, a plasma treatment provides manifold possibilities to refine a polymer surface, enabled by the adjustment of parameters like

- Gas flows (50%),
- Power (50%),
- Pressure (starting from 886 pa to 50 pa)
- Treatment time (30 seconds).

2.1.2 Rinsing

After the washing step, the yarns have been rinsed with distilled water and dried (wih a hair dryer).

2.1.3 Polymerization

2.1.3.1 Preparation of Polypyrrole (PPy) solution

For the polymerization reaction, first a 0.04M PPy solution has been used.

- 0.71 ml/250 ml of PPy

It was necessary to use 0.71 ml of PPy and filled up with distilled water till we had 250 ml in the slops(PPy was well mixed with water). After that the yarn were placed in the solution for 1 hour at room temperature.

2.1.3.2 Preparation of $FeCl_3$–BSA (Benzene Sulphonic Acid) solution

The solution contains:

- $FeCl_3$ -- 6.43 g/250 ml
- BSA-- 0.54 g/250 ml

It was weighed out 6.43 g/250 ml of $FeCl_3$ and 0.54 g/250 ml of BSA and dissolved them in 250 ml of distilled water. This solution was added to the yarn in the Pyrrole solution and the polymerization was carried out at least 1 hour at $5^0 C$.

The polymerization was stopped when the color of the solution and the yarn changed into a very dark greenish color.

2.1.4 Rinsing

The Polypyrrole coated yarn was rinsed with distilled water until no coating residues are visible on the yarn and rinsing water appeared clear in color.

2.1.5 Drying

The yarns were dried by using a hair dryer.

2.2 Resistance Measurement at different lengths for coating with Polypyrrole

Polyamide 6.10; Diameter: **0.220 mm**

[Table 1: Resistances in MΩ after Polypyrrole coating]

Sample	Lengths		
	3 cm	**6 cm**	**9 cm**
1	0.95	1.55	2.64
2	1.1426	2.145	2.801
3	0.8023	1.482	2.077
Average	0.965	1.726	2.506

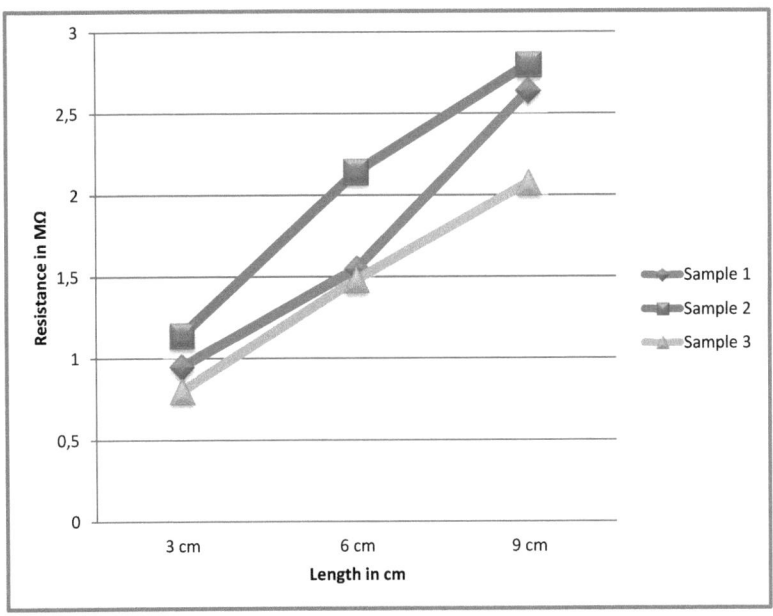

Figure 2: Resistances Measurement for Polypyrrole Coating

2.3 Resistance Measurement at different lengths for coating with Polypyrrole(PPy)

Polyester PET 930C; Diameter: **0.550 mm**

[Table 2: Resistances in MΩ after Polypyrrole coating]

Sample	Lengths		
	3 cm	**6 cm**	**9 cm**
1	0.2385	0.4980	0.6842
2	0.2862	0.5380	0.8436
3	0.2409	0.4204	0.6366
Average	0.2552	0.4855	0.7215

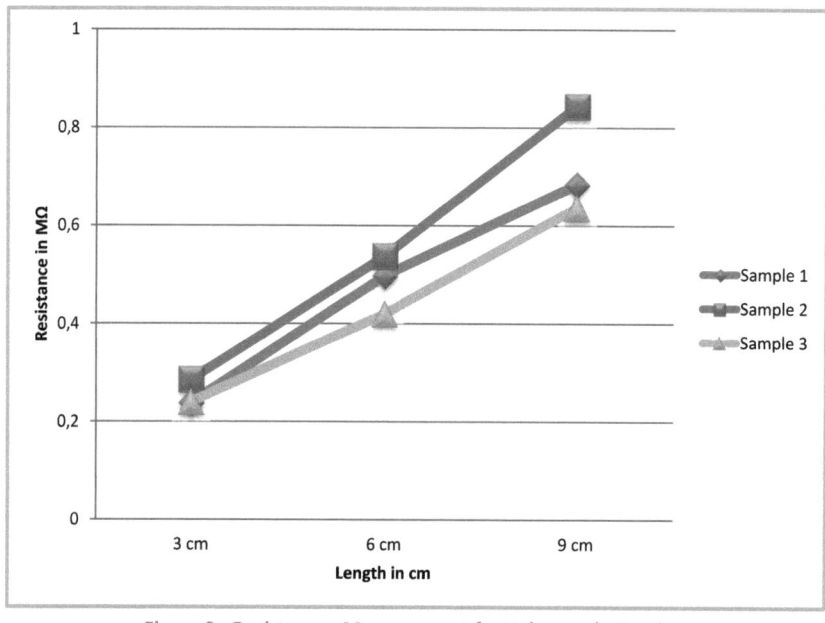

Figure 3: Resistances Measurement for Polypyrrole Coating

2.4 Resistance Measurement at different lengths for coating with Polypyrrole(PPy)

Polyester PETP Monofilament; Diameter: **0.650 mm**

[Table 3: : Resistances in MΩ after Polypyrrole coating]

Sample	Lengths		
	3 cm	**6 cm**	**9 cm**
1	0.214	0.4204	0.5943
2	0.1753	0.3875	0.5605
3	0.1664	0.3538	0.5149
Average	0.1852	0.3872	0.5566

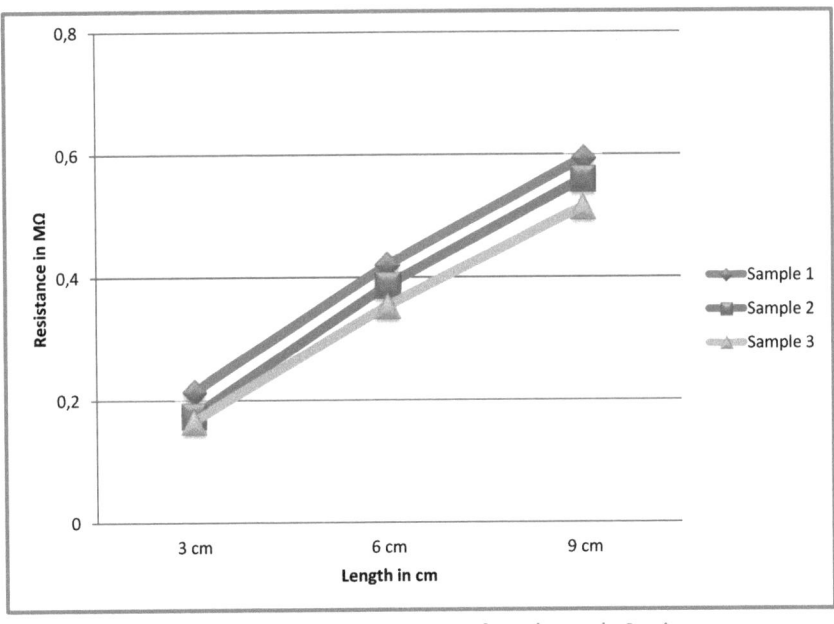

Figure 4: Resistances Measurement for Polypyrrole Coating

2.5 Resistance Measurement at different lengths for coating with Polypyrrole (PPy)

Polyester PET 930R Monofilament; Diameter: **0.650 mm**

[Table 4: Resistances in MΩ after Polypyrrole coating]

Sample	Lengths		
	3 cm	**6 cm**	**9 cm**
1	2.063	10.48	12.16
2	0.69	1.46	2.2
3	0	3.20	4.76
Average	0.918	5.047	2.506

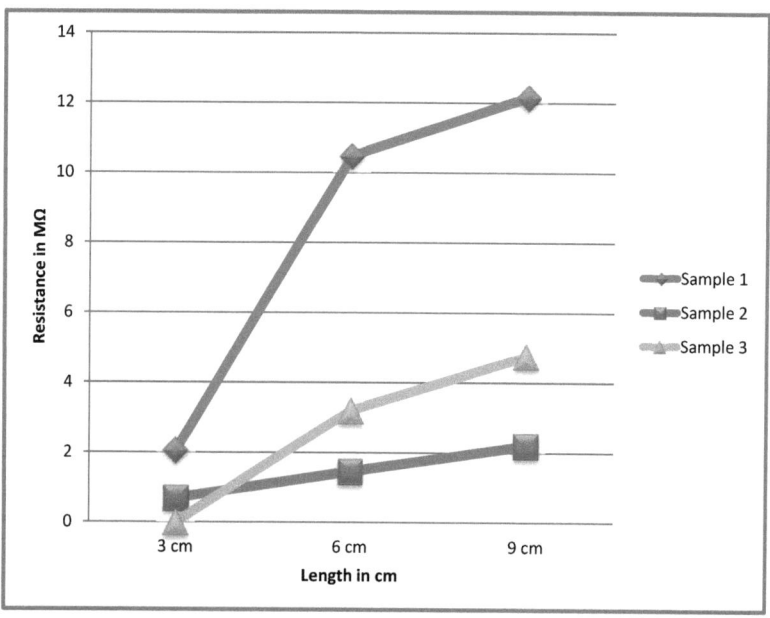

Figure 5: Resistances Measurement for Polypyrrole Coating

2.6 Optical Microscopic Views

Polypyrrole Coating

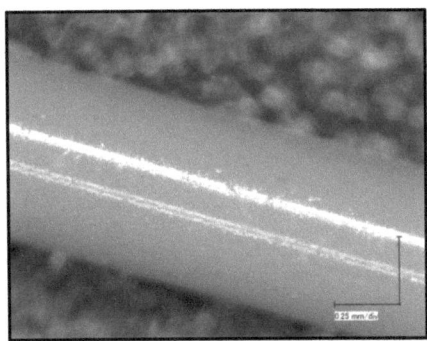 

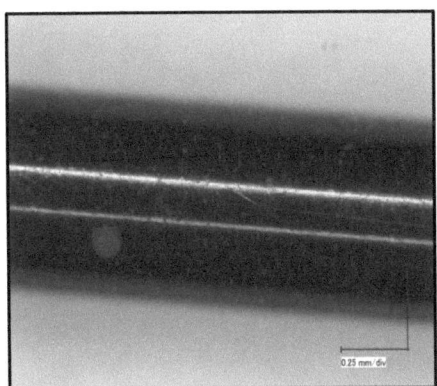 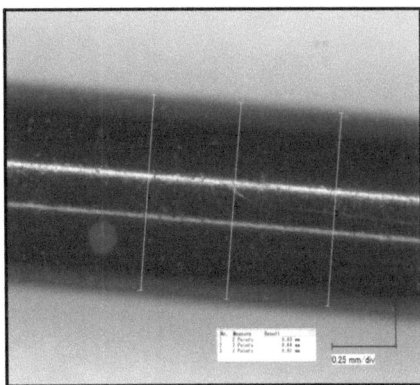

Figure 6: Polyester PETP Monofilament; Diameter: 0.650 mm before and after Polypyrrole coating

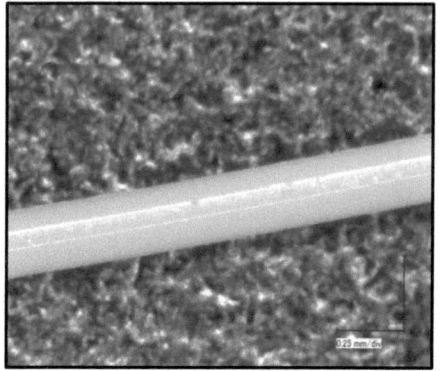 

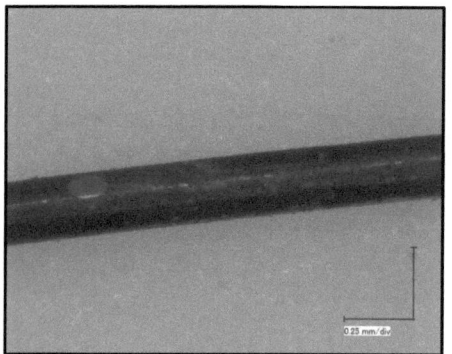 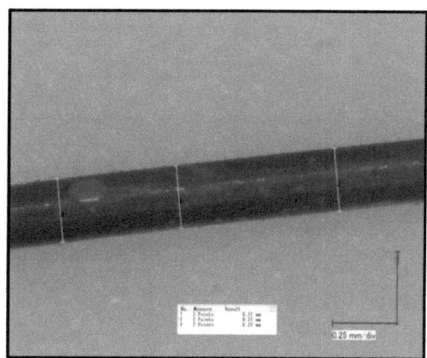

Figure 7: Polyamide 6.10; Diameter: **0.220 mm** before and after Polypyrrole coating

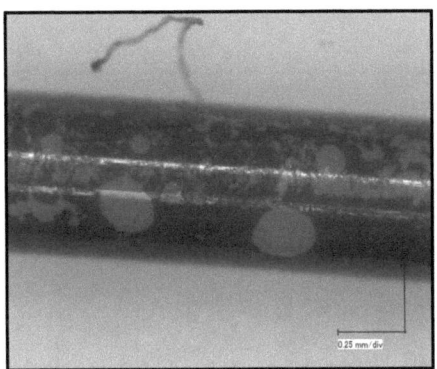 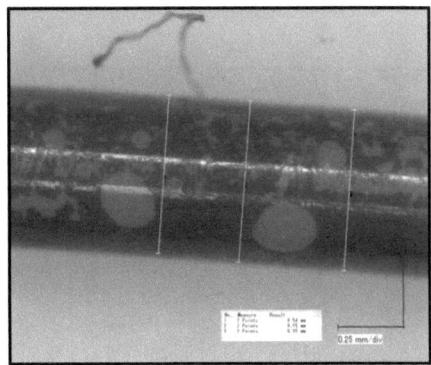

Figure 8: Polyester PET 930C; Diameter: 0.550 mm before and after Polypyrrole coating

Figure 9: Polyester PET 930R Monofilament; Diameter: 0.650 mm before and after
Polypyrrole coating

2.7 Electron Microscopic Views

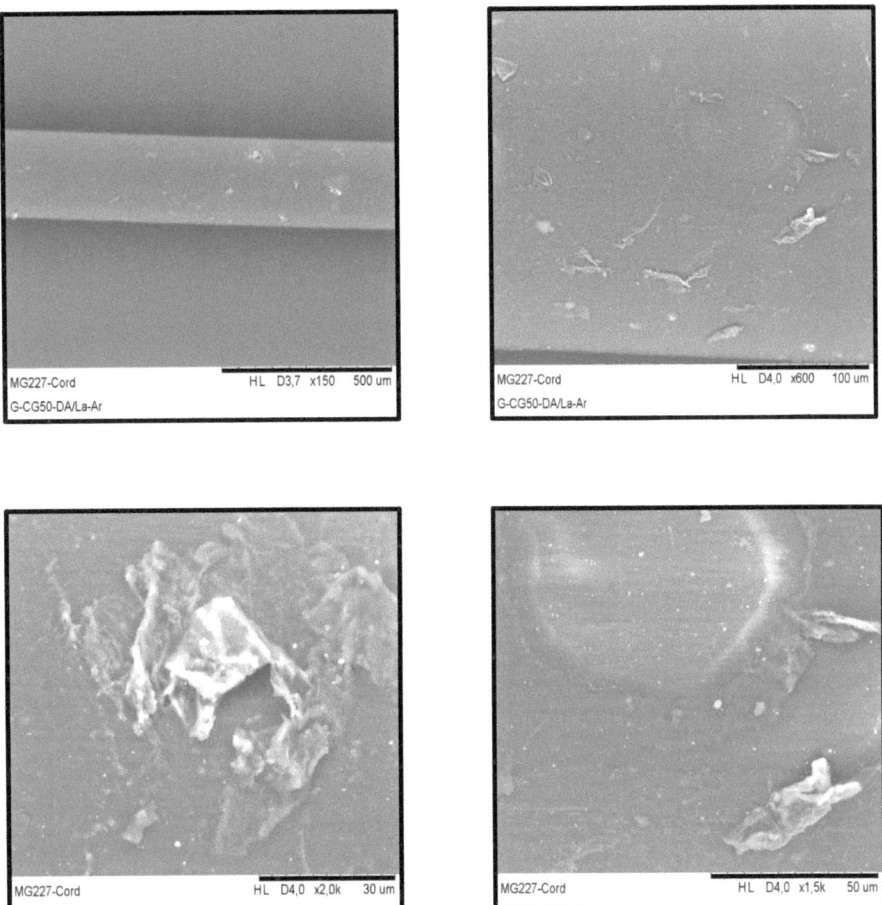

Figure 10: Polyamide 6.10; Diameter: 0.220 mm after Polypyrrole coating

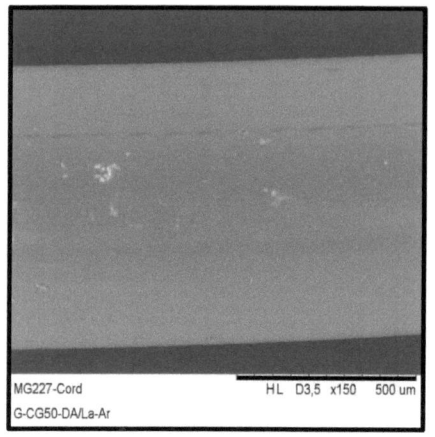
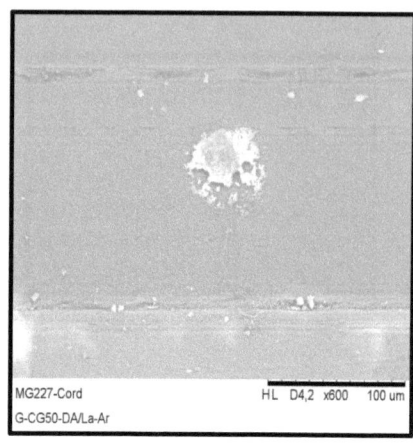
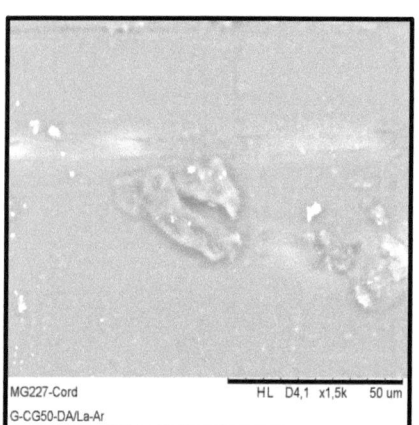
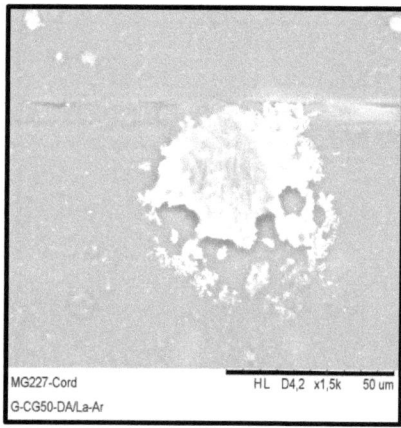

Figure 11: Polyester PET 930R; Diameter: 0.650 mm after Polypyrrole coating

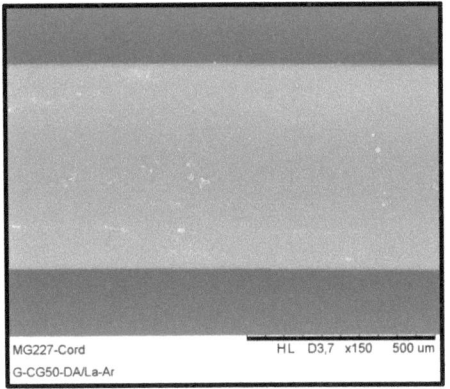
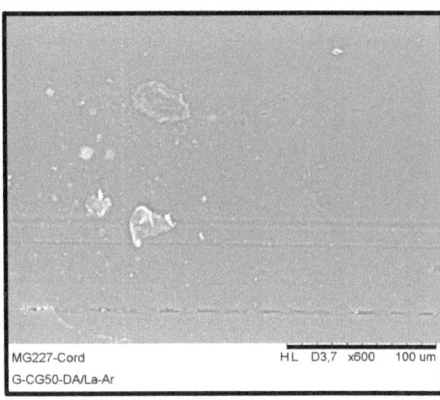

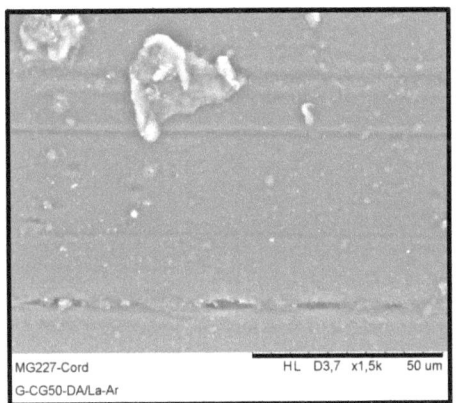
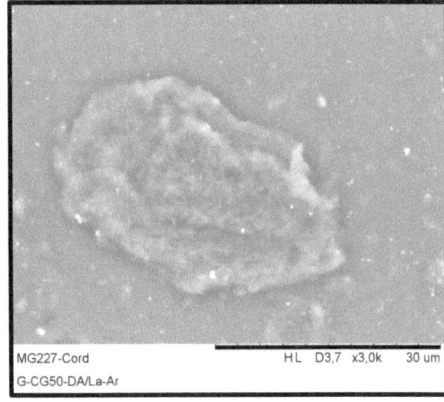

Figure 12: Polyester PET 930C; Diameter: 0.550 mm after Polypyrrole coating

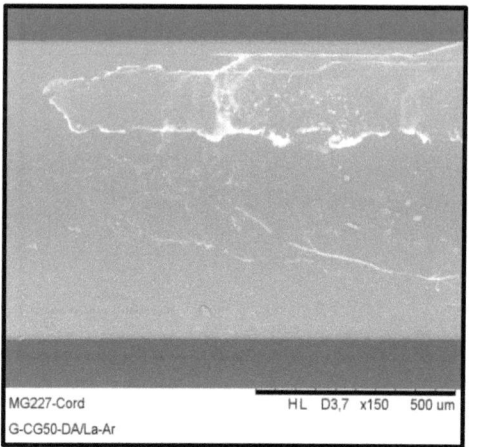
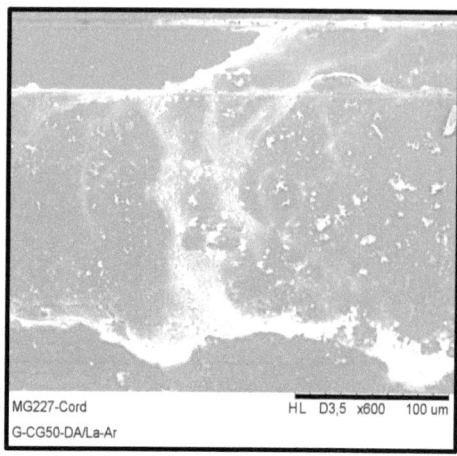

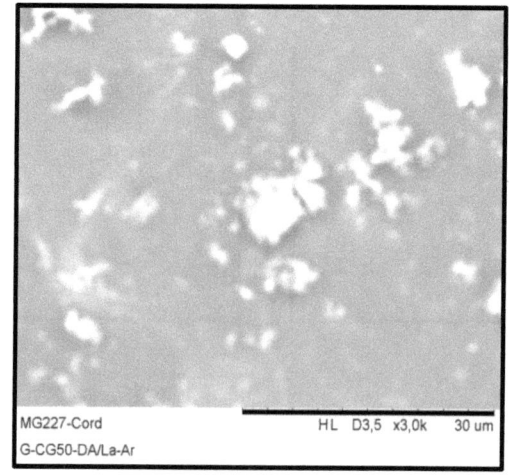

Figure 13: Polyester PETP Monofilament; Diameter: 0.650 mm after Polypyrrole coating

Chapter III
Dip Coating of Yarns with Carbon
(Graphite)

3.1 Carbon (Graphite) Dip Coating Procedure

3.1.1 Plasma Treatment

As yarns used for this project work are synthetic and have low coating adhesion so plasma treatment has done.

The Plasma Treatment Process consists of exposing a polymer to a low-temperature, high density glow discharge. Primarily, a plasma treatment provides manifold possibilities to refine a polymer surface, enabled by the adjustment of parameters like

- Gas flows (50%),
- Power (50%),
- Pressure (starting from 886 pa to 50 pa)
- Treatment time (30 seconds).

3.1.2 Preparation of Solution

Graphite Flakes Powder
- Very pure and very fine
- Type: MA-296
- Fineness: 75 μm
- Company: NGS Nature Graphite

For dip coating **15%** solution was prepared.

The solution contains:

- Graphite—15g
- Binder—85 g

Both Graphite and Binder were mixed very well by stirring until it would turn into a semi solid form. When the solution was ready, the beaker was put in the Dip Coating machine.

Figure 14 &15: Dip Coating Machine

3.1.3 Machine Operation:

The samples of yarns were clamped individually by the clamp of machine.

Then 3 samples were taken to coat at different speeds.

- 50 mm/min
- 100 mm/min
- 150 mm/min

3.2 Resistance Measurement at different speeds for Dip Coating with Carbon (Graphite)

Polyester PET 930C; Diameter: **0.550 mm**

Table 5: Resistances in KΩ after dip coating

Speed in mm/min	Length- 2 cm
50	82.5
100	10.6
150	21.6

Polyamide 6.10; Diameter: **0.220 mm**

Table 6: Resistances in KΩ after dip coating

Speed in mm/min	Length- 2 cm
50	0
100	0
150	0

Polyester PETP Monofilament; Diameter: **0.650 mm**

Table 7: Resistances in KΩ after dip coating

Speed in mm/min	Length- 2 cm
50	29.5
100	6.2
150	8.5

Polyester PET 930R Monofilament; Diameter: **0.650 mm**

Table 8: Resistances in KΩ after dip coating

Speed in mm/min	Length- 2 cm
50	18.5
100	9.3
150	14.5

3.3 Dip Coating of Yarns with Carbon (Graphite)

Electron Microscopic Views

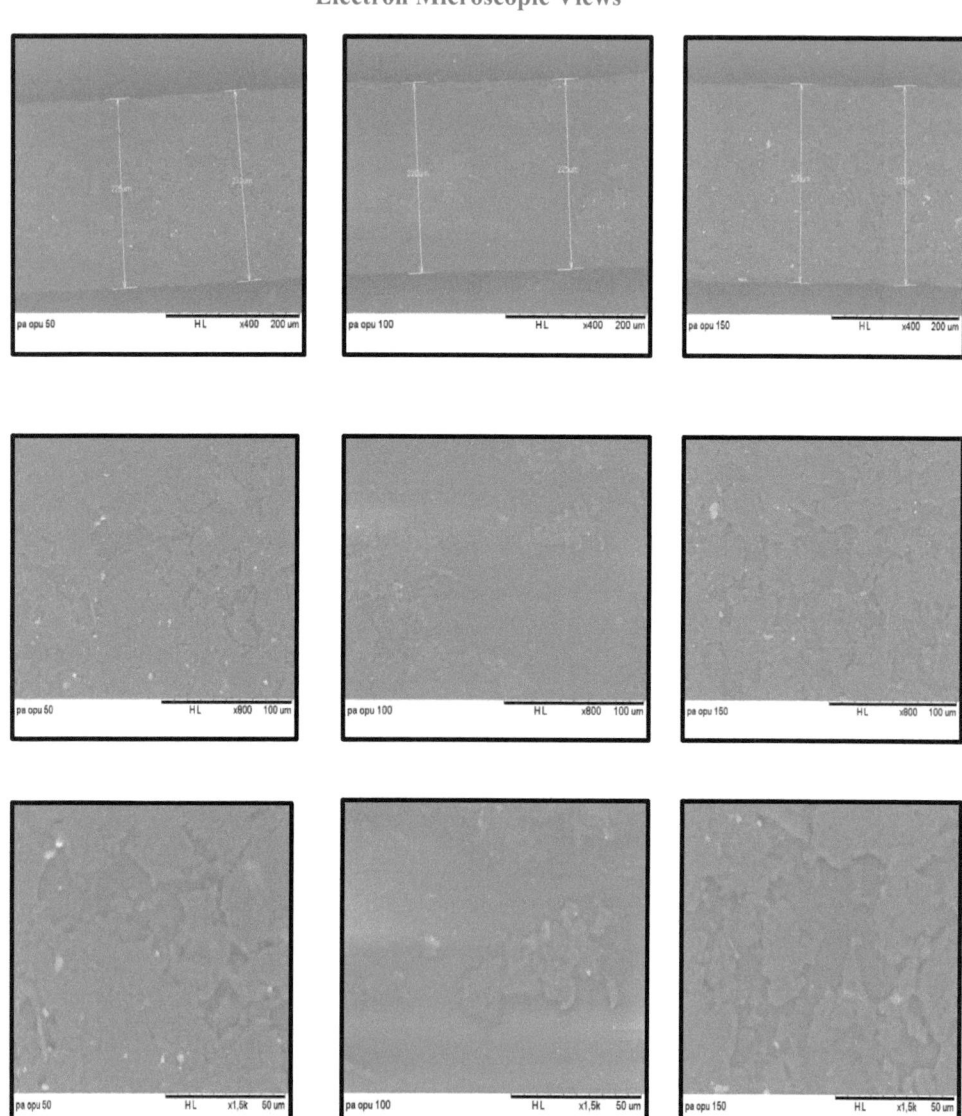

Figure 16: Polyamide 6.10; Diameter: **0.220 mm after Carbon (Graphite) Dip coating**

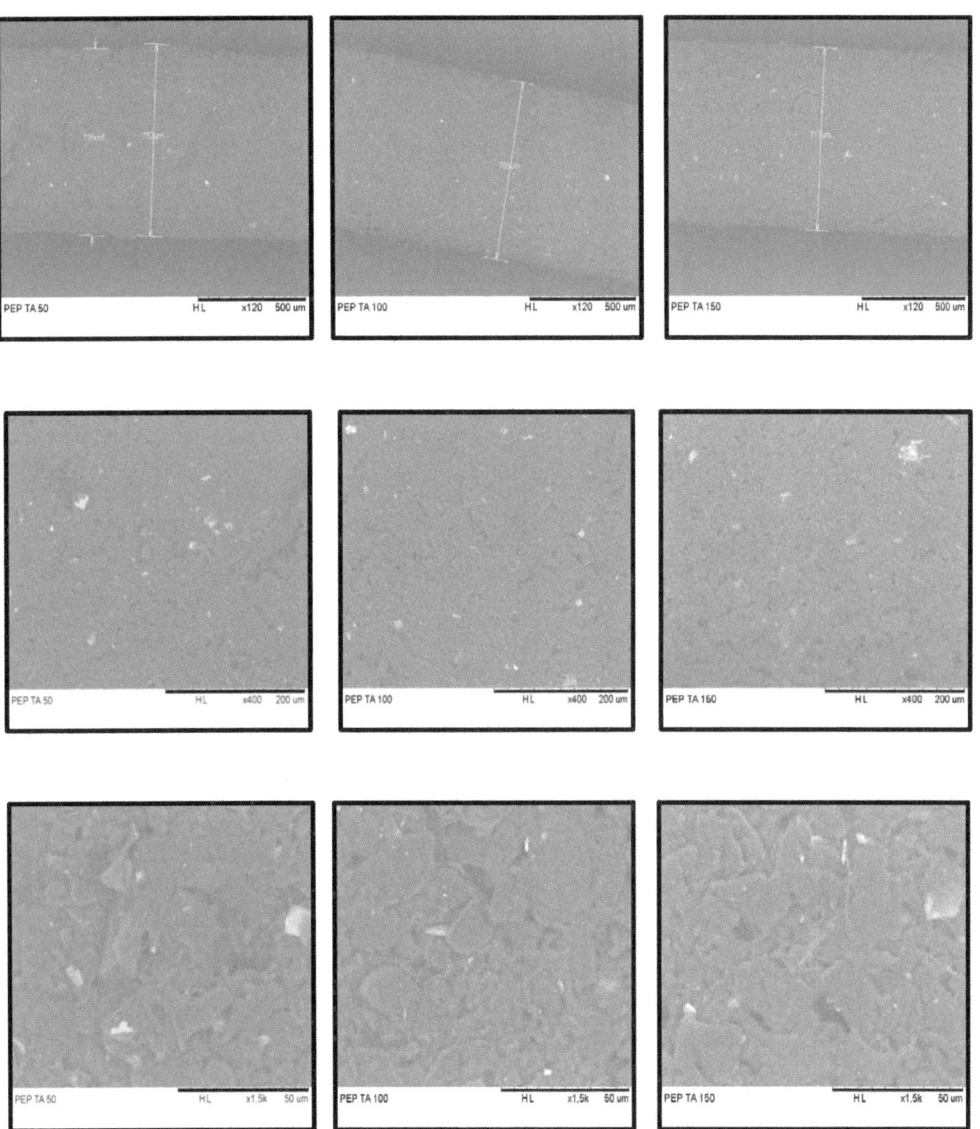

Figure 17: Polyester PETP; Diameter: **0.650 mm after Carbon (Graphite) Dip coating**

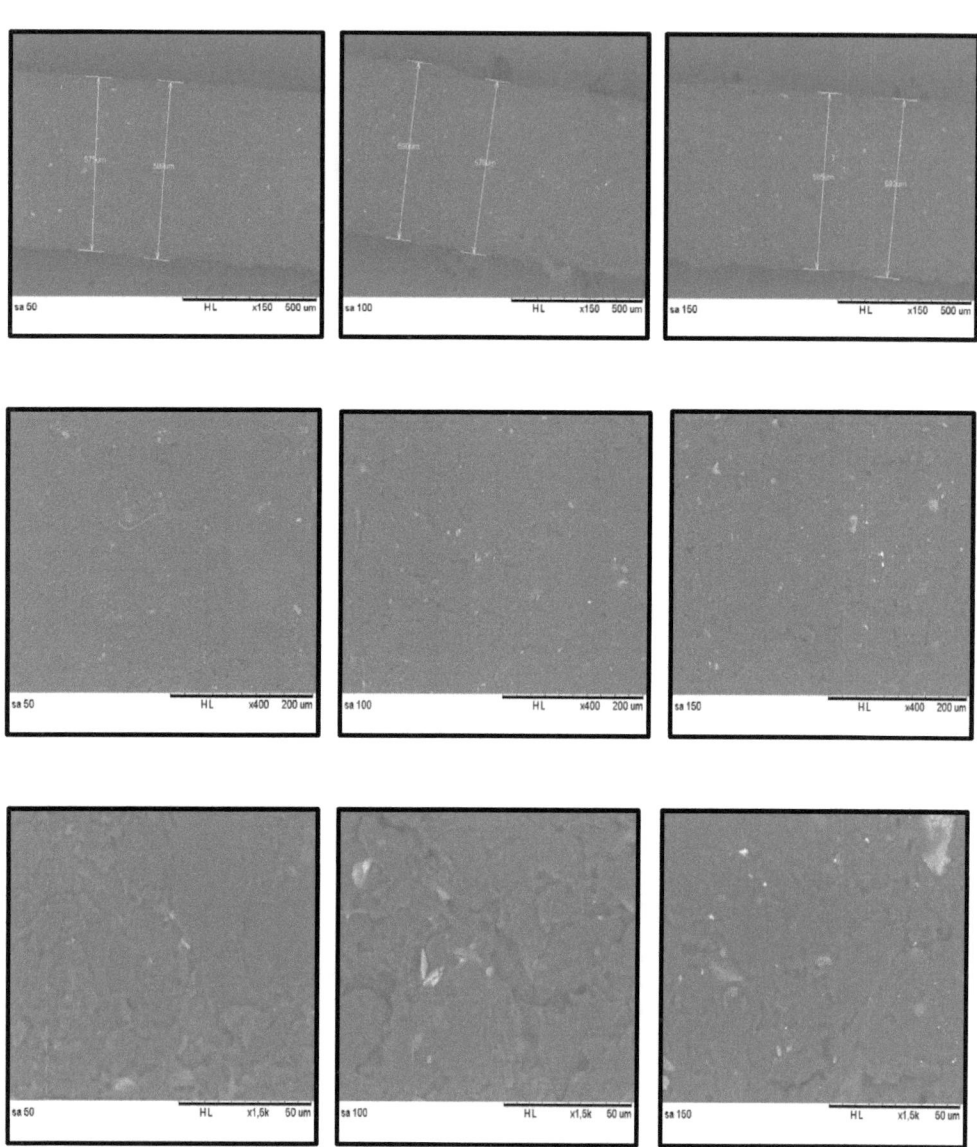

Figure 18: Polyester PET 930C; Diameter: 0.550mm after Carbon (Graphite) Dip coating

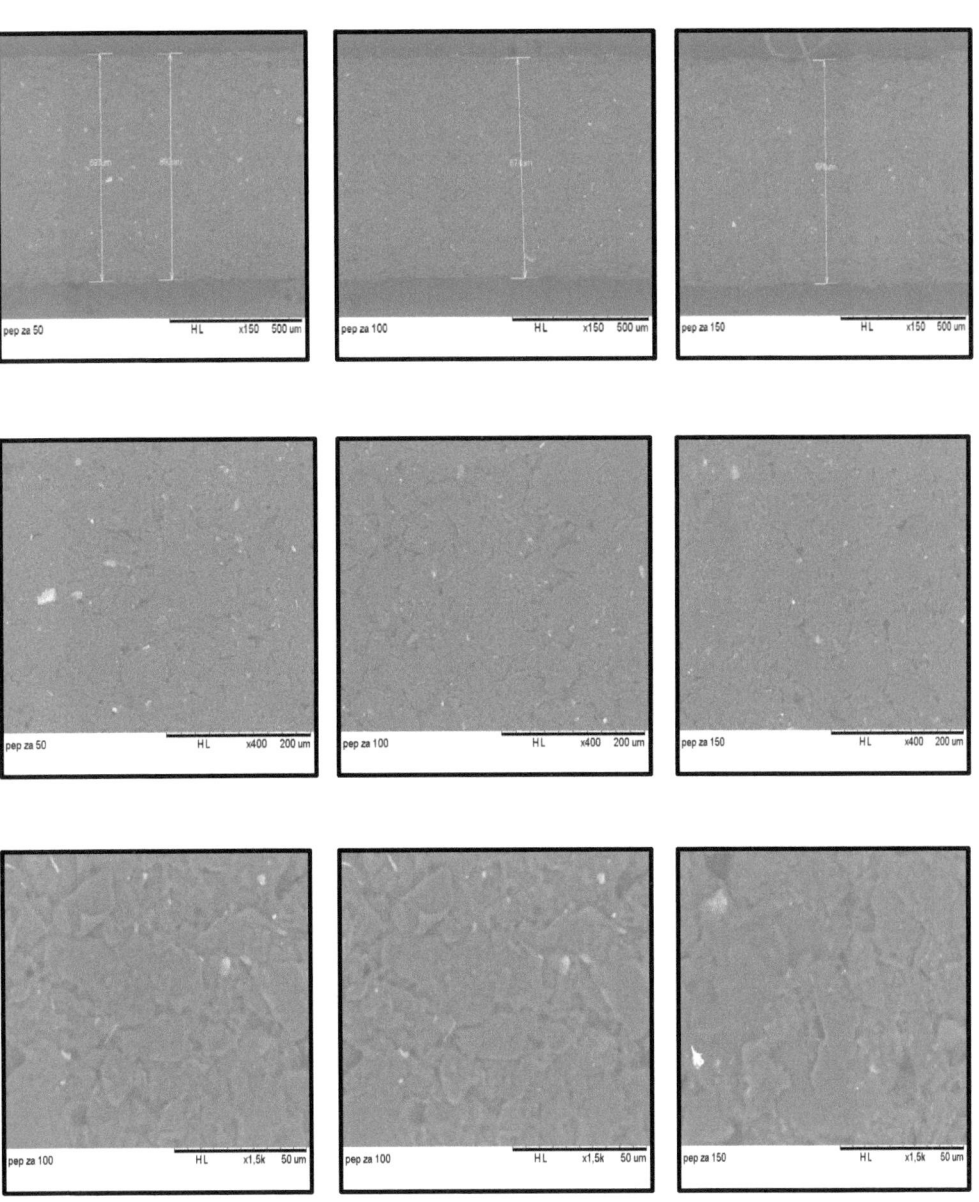

Figure 19: Polyester PET 930R; Diameter: **0.650 mm** after Carbon (Graphite) Dip coating

Chapter IV
Characterization of Yarns

4.1 Comparison of Coated and Uncoated Yarns after Polypyrrole Coating

Table 9: Differences in diameters in mm

Yarns	Diameters in mm		
	Uncoated	Coated	Differences
PA	0.220	0.231	0.011
PETP	0.650	0.669	0.019
PET 930C	0.550	0.562	0.012
PET 930R	0.650	0.663	0.013

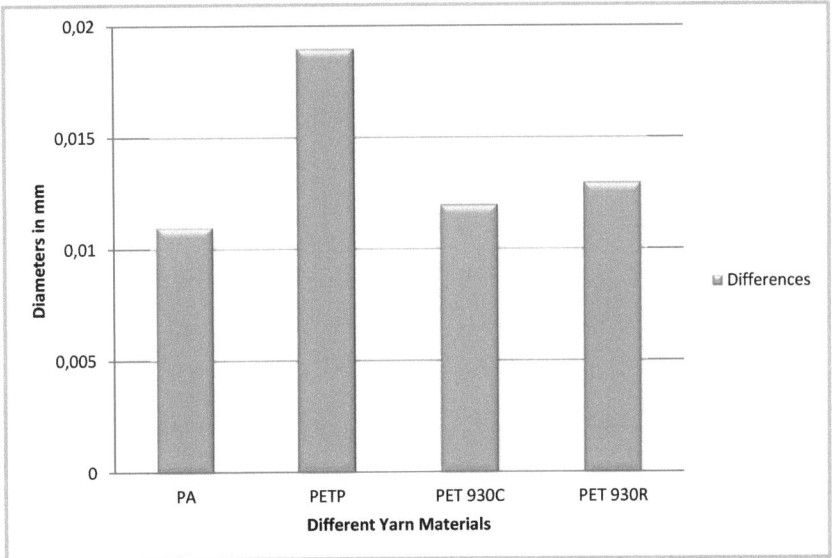

Figure 20: Differences in diameters after Polypyrrole coating

From Figure-20 it can be easily said that after coating of yarns with Polypyrrole the diameter of yarns increased. Actually different yarn materials have been used, which did not make any great impact in case of increasing diameter after coating. If closely notice at the values of diameters, the increase is very little, only because those yarn materials are synthetic. That means those yarn have very little coating adhesion to of chemicals/water than natural fibers like: Cotton, Wool, Silk etc.

4.2 Comparison of Uncoated and Coated Diameters after Coating with Carbon (Graphite)

Table 10: Diameters measured at different speeds

Speed	Diameters in mm							
	PA		PETP		PET 930C		PET 930R	
	Uncoated	Coated	Uncoated	Coated	Uncoated	Coated	Uncoated	Coated
50 mm/min	0.220	0.226	0.650	0.744	0.550	0.582	0.650	0.695
100 mm/min	0.220	0.225	0.650	0.703	0.550	0.584	0.650	0.674
150 mm/min	0.220	0.237	0.650	0.717	0.550	0.589	0.650	0.685

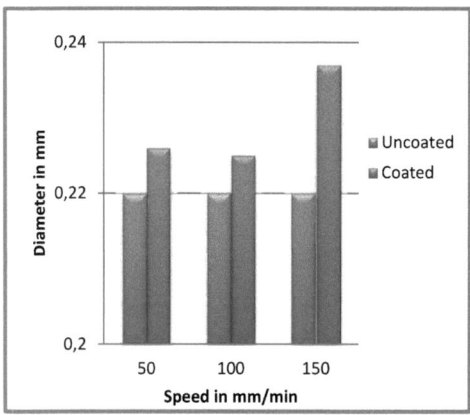

Figure 21: Polyamide (PA)

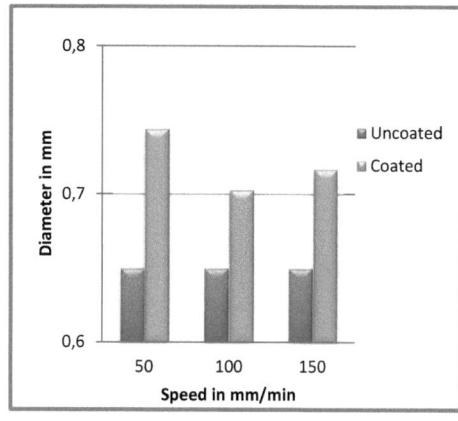

Figure 22: Polyester (PETP)

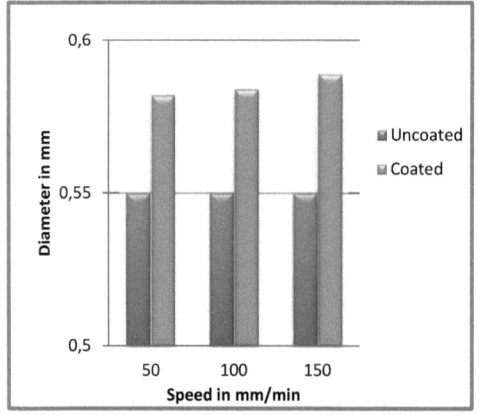

Figure 23: Polyester (PET)

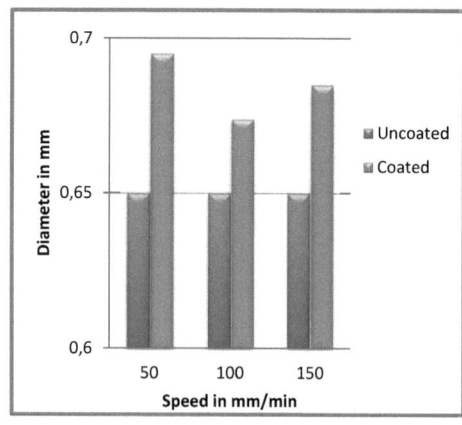

Figure 24: Polyester (PET 930R)

33

From the figure-21, 22, 23 and 24 it is seen that after coating of yarns with Carbon (Graphite) the diameter of yarns were increased. Values in the Table-10 show that PETP yarn has higher and PA has lower increase in diameter than other yarns if those are compared with uncoated ones.

4.3 Comparison of Diameters among Yarns after Coating with Carbon (Graphite)

Table 11: Diameters after dip coating

Speed	Diameters in mm			
	PA	PETP	PET 930C	PET 930R
50 mm/min	0.226	0.744	0.582	0.695
100 mm/min	0.225	0.703	0.584	0.674
150 mm/min	0.237	0.717	0.589	0.685

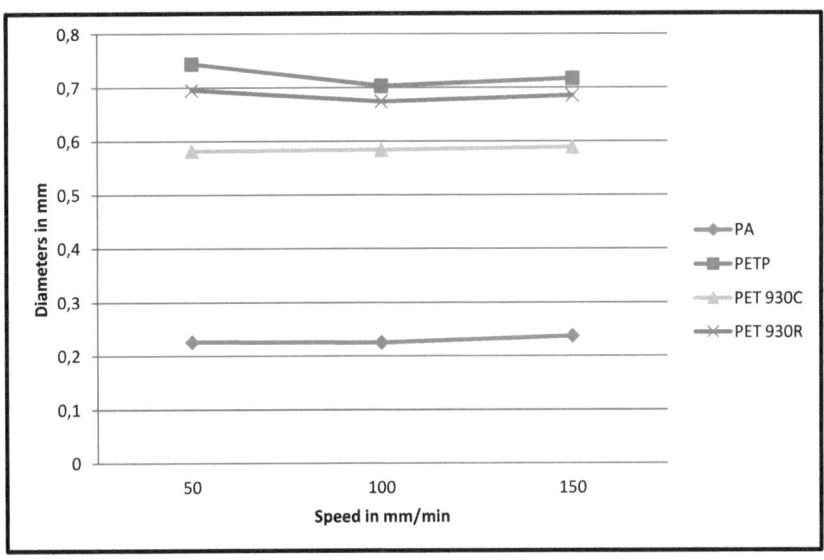

Figure 25: Comparison of Diameters among yarns after Coating with Carbon (Graphite)

From the Figure-25, it is clear that different yarn materials have different type of absorbency. That's why their chemical uptakes are different. Here speed of the machine also plays an important role. As all these yarn materials are man-made, in the Graph-10 the lines are showing almost same characteristics for different speeds. But from the values of Table-10 and 11, PA has very little coating adhesion comparing to other yarns. On the other hand

PETP has very high uptake of chemicals and PET 930C and PET 930R also have very good uptake.

4.4 Comparison of Different Yarn Resistances after Polypyrrole Coating

Table 12: Resistances in MΩ

Yarns	Lengths		
	3 cm	6 cm	9 cm
PA	0.965	1.726	2.506
PETP	0.2552	0.4855	0.7215
PET 930C	0.1852	0.3872	0.5566
PET 930R	0.918	5.047	2.506

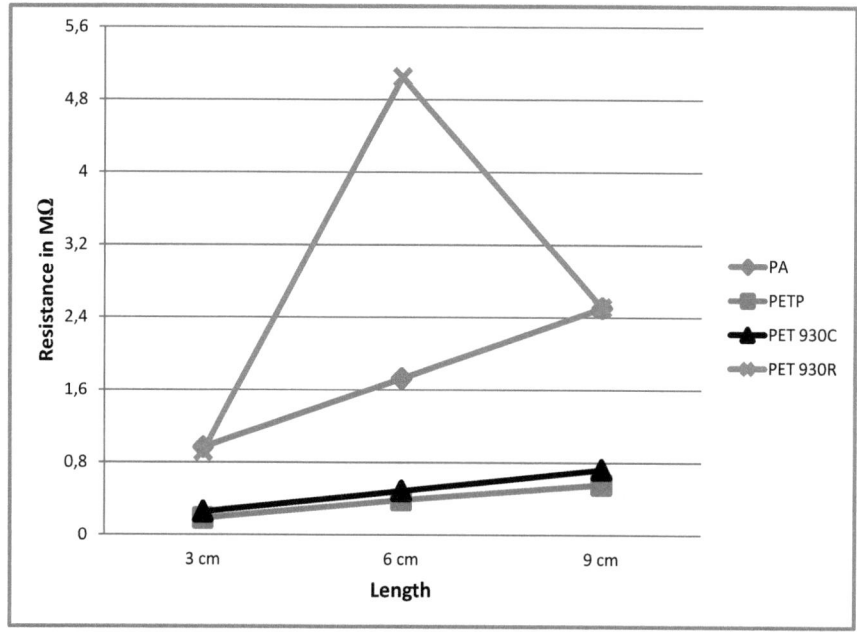

Figure 26: Comparison of Different Yarn Resistances after Polypyrrole Coating

After coating with Polypyrrole from figure-26, it is visible that with the increase in measurement length, resistances are also increased for all yarns except PET 930R yarn.

4.5 Comparison of Different Yarn Resistances after Carbon (Graphite) Dip Coating

Speed in mm/min	Length- 2 cm			
	PETP	**PA**	**PET 930R**	**PET 930C**
50	29.5	0	18.5	82.5
100	6.2	0	9.3	10.6
150	8.5	0	14.5	21.6

Table 13: Resistances in KΩ after dip coating

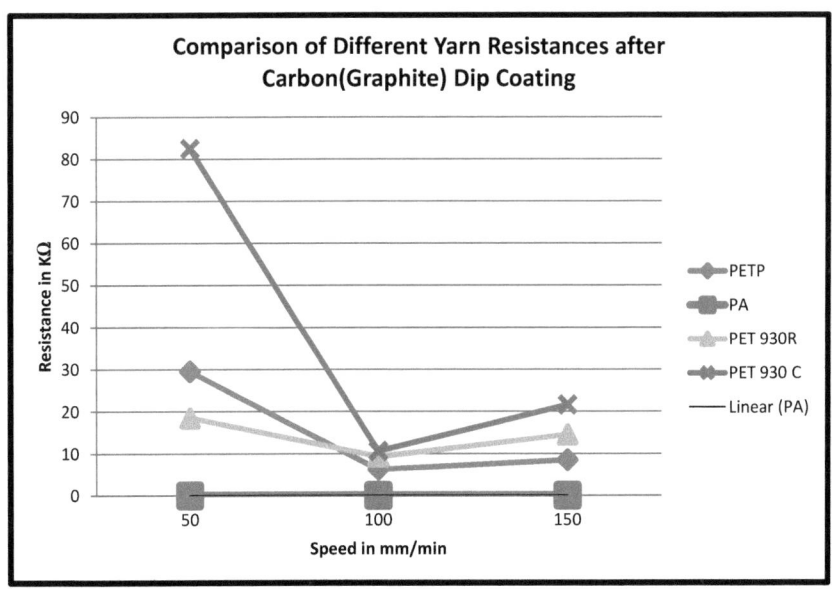

Figure 27: Comparison of Different Yarn Resistances after Carbon(Graphite) Dip Coating

From figure-27, it can be said that after coating with Carbon (Graphite), PA shows no conductivity even in change of speeds. While PET 930C has shown great resistivity but it also fluctuated in different speeds. Other two yarns have variations in resistance.

Chapter V
Results and Discussions

5.1 Conductivity

As our main aim was to make the yarn materials conductive by electro active layers, we applied Polypyrrole and Carbon (Graphite) coating on four different yarn materials.

5.1.1 For Polypyrrole Coating

For this type of coating, resistance is measured in three different lengths which are 3cm, 6cm and 9 cm to check the variations. All the yarns have showed increase in resistance as the lengths of measurement were increased.

Because according to **Pouillet's Law**

$$R \propto \frac{l}{A}$$

In above formula,
R = Resistance in ohms [Ω]
l = Length in meter
A = Cross sectional area in m^2
Here resistance is proportional to length and inversely proportional to cross sectional area. That means if length is increased then resistance will also be increased according to this law. [15] Values of Table-12 are showing this occurrence.

All the yarns showed gradual increase in resistance except Polyester PET 930R yarn. At 6 cm length its resistance value was higher than 9 cm. This type of occurrence happens if coating is not uniform.
Comparing all yarn materials, Polyamide (PA) has more resistance increase than others. It means conductivity will be lower than other as well. But similarly Polyester PET 930R has also good resistance like PA. Other two yarns Polyester PETP and Polyester PET 930C have lower resistance. That means they are good conductor of electricity after Polypyrrole coating.

5.1.2 For Carbon (Graphite) Coating

In a dip-coating process, a substrate is dipped into a liquid coating solution and then is withdrawn from the solution at a controlled speed. Coating thickness generally increases with faster withdrawal speed. The thickness is determined by the balance of forces at the stagnation point on the liquid surface. A faster withdrawal speed pulls more fluid up onto the surface of the substrate before it has time to flow back down into the solution. The thickness is primarily affected by fluid viscosity, fluid density, and surface tension. [13]

Dip coating technology was used to make the yarn materials conductive. For this coating process three different speeds of machines were used which are 50 mm/min, 100 mm/min and 150 mm/min to check how the speed and time make impact on conductivity of yarns. Table-13 shows the differences.

Polyamide (PA) yarn showed no conductivity for all the different speeds. This is because of low chemical uptake of the material. So this type of coating is not good enough for PA.

According to **Landau and Levich equation,**

$$H = \frac{0.94\ (\mu \vartheta)^{2/3}}{\gamma^{1/6}.(\rho.g)^{1/2}}$$

H= Thickness; μ = fluid viscosity; v = withdrawal speed; ρ = fluid density; g = gravitational acceleration; γ = surface tension (liquid-air) [14]

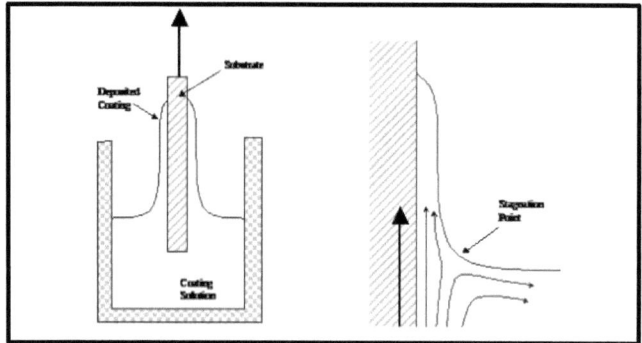

Figure 28: Schematic diagram of Dip coating process [13]

According to above equation if speed is increased then thickness or coating will also be increased.

In the Table-13; for 150 mm/min speed, the resistance values are higher than 100 mm/min for all the yarn materials except PA. That means yarn materials which are coated at 150 mm/min speed should have thicker coating and higher resistance with lower conductivity than yarns which were coated at 100 mm/min speed and after coating got the same result.

But for slower speed at 50 mm/min showed something different which was not following the rule. At this speed resistance values are so high that means those yarns are less conductive.

So yarns which were coated at 100 mm/min are more conductive among all other speeds except PA yarn.

PA yarn has very low water and chemical uptake than other types of Polyester fibers. Because it has higher hydrophobic properties. That's why it showed almost no adhesion to coating chemicals and no resistivity as well and may be this type of coating is not appropriate for PA.

5.2 Yarn Diameter

Coating also made great changes in yarn diameters.

5.2.1 For Polypyrrole Coating

Table-9 shows variation of diameters of uncoated and coated yarns. For Polyester PETP the diameter increase is more than other yarns. That means this yarn material has good adhesion of coating chemicals especially for Polypyrrole. Other yarns have similar increase in diameter.

5.2.2 For Carbon (Graphite) Coating

From Table-10, as for dip coating three different speeds were used, PA and PET 930C have more increase in diameter in the speed of 150 mm/min. On the other hand PET 930R and PETP yarns showed increase in case of 50 mm/min speed.

All these variations occurred because of different adhesion ability by yarns of coating chemicals and viscosity of solution as well.

Chapter VI
Drawbacks

6.1 Limitations of Project Work

Despite of good laboratory facilities, this type of project work requires lot of time to do experiments especially like Polypyrrole coating and Carbon (Graphite) dip coating. First of all the experiments have to be finished and then some physical and chemical tests needed to be done. There was not enough time to do everything properly in the limited time. Because experiments are something that could not give the desired results all the time and may be needed to do that again. So for this reason lot of things could not be done as planned at the beginning.

Chapter VII
Conclusions

7.1 Conclusions

Accuracy of the results of this project work is not over question due to having some limitations though it was tried best to overcome all constraints. But lack of time instead of great laboratory facilities may hamper the desired results sometimes about making the yarns conductive. So a further research work with good planning is recommended.

Bibliography

1. http://www.apexicindia.com/en/technologies/dip-coating-technology
2. http://www.scienceclarified.com/Di-El/Electrical-Conductivity.html
3. Materials Sciences and Applications, 2010, 1, 253-259
4. Polypyrrole formation and use by Paul Saville, January 2005
5. http://en.wikipedia.org/wiki/Carbon
6. http://en.wikipedia.org/wiki/graphite
7. Electrically conductive coatings of nickel and polypyrrole/poly(2-methoxyaniline-5-sulfonicacid) on nylon Lycra® textiles, University of Wollongong, research online.
8. Characterization of Conductive Polypyrrole Coated Wool Yarns, Fibers and Polymers 2002, Vol.3, No.1, 24-30.
9. http://en.wikipedia.org/wiki/Polypyrrole
10. http://www.preservearticles.com/201012291918/properties-and-uses-of-graphite.html
11. http://scholar.google.de/
12. Polypyrrole Coated PET Fabrics for Thermal Applications: *Materials Sciences and Applications*, 2010, 1, 253-259
13. http://www.ytca.com/dip_coating
14. http://www.apexicindia.com/en/technologies/dip-coating-technology
15. http://www.physindex.com/e/Pouillet's%20law/
16. http://www.textileworld.com/Issues/2005/November-December/Dyeing_Printing_and_Finishing/The_Plasma_Advantage
17. www.fibtex.lodz.pl/2012/1/56.pdf